MAHALIA JACKSON

WALKING with KINGS and QUEENS

by NINA NOLAN

illustrated by JOHN HOLYFIELD

Amistad

An Imprint of HarperCollinsPublishers

Amistad is an imprint of HarperCollins Publishers.
Mahalia Jackson
Text copyright © 2015 by Nina Nolan
Illustrations copyright © 2015 by John Holyfield
All rights reserved. Manufactured in China.

Library of Congress Cataloging-in-Publication Data
Nolan, Nina.
 Mahalia Jackson : walking with Kings and Queens / by Nina Nolan ;
illustrations by John Holyfield. — First edition.
  pages cm
 Audience: Age 5–10.
 Audience: Grade K to grade 3.
 ISBN 978-0-06-087944-0 (hardcover) — ISBN 978-0-06-087945-7 (library)
 1. Jackson, Mahalia, 1911–1972—Juvenile literature. 2. Gospel musicians—
United States—Biography—Juvenile literature. I. Holyfield, John, illustrator.
II. Title.
ML3930.J2N65 2015   2013051288
782.25'4092—dc23   CIP
                                                                             [B]

The art for this book was painted with acrylic on paper.
Typography by Sarah Creech
14 15 16 17 18 SCP 10 9 8 7 6 5 4 3 2 1
❖
First Edition

To my mother, Reetie —N.N.

To the memories of my grandmothers,
Gracie Holyfield and Ruby Wilkinson,
for their devoted love and encouragement — J.H.

People might say little Mahalia Jackson was born with nothing, but she had *something* all right. A voice that was bigger than she was.

It was New Orleans, and music was everywhere. Blues spilling through windows. Jazz pouring out doors.

But it was gospel that Mahalia loved.

After her mother died, Mahalia was sent to live with her aunt Duke. Her aunt was very strict, especially with her white-glove test on Mahalia's dusting.

But singing in church raised her spirits.
She felt like a peacock with her feathers
all spread out.

In the fourth grade, Mahalia had to leave school to look after her baby cousins. She would drag out the record player and sing along. Her voice settled the babies. People walking by stopped in their tracks to listen.

"Don't you worry," her aunt Bell said as Mahalia shucked peas on the front porch. "One day you'll walk with kings and queens." How was Mahalia going to walk with kings and queens? She didn't even have shoes. But Aunt Bell had a way of *knowing* things.

Over the next few years, Mahalia kept singing in church, spreading her peacock feathers. And every chance she got, she worked as a maid and saved her money. She kept hearing about people moving to Chicago. Sounded scary. All those gangsters. But people said there were more chances there, too. Maybe even a chance to go back to school.

When Mahalia was sixteen, her aunt Hannah visited from Chicago. "Want to come back with me?" she asked. Train was leaving in the morning. No time to lose. Music had always helped calm Mahalia, but this was a new song. *Clickety-clack. Clickety-clack.* Two days on the train. She was a bundle of nerves.

Everything about Chicago felt strange.
It wasn't just the bigness of it all.
Or that *wind*.
It was everything.
Mahalia could get a coat to warm her
outsides. But she'd have to find a church
to warm her insides. A church to sing in.

She found a church all right. And a school, too.
Things were looking up in Chicago.

When Aunt Hannah got sick, Mahalia had to stop
school to work. Back to being a maid. Again.
But she kept on singing.

A few times, Mahalia went to hear a band play in a nightclub. It wasn't gospel, but the music sure did sound good.

But when Grandpa had a heart attack, Mahalia made a promise to God. "If you let Grandpa get better, I'll never set foot in a nightclub again." Grandpa got better. And that was that.

People kept telling Mahalia if she would sing in nightclubs, instead of churches, she'd make enough money to quit working as a maid. Those people could say what they wanted. Mahalia knew what *she* said to God.

She drove down South, singing in churches. It was for money now, but not much, and only sometimes.

Mahalia kept driving on those may-blow tires: tires so bald, they may blow any minute. No money to fix them. Keep singing and driving.

Mahalia's joyful voice lifted people with hope. After she sang in a church, people lined up to join the congregation.

When she finally had money for a singing lesson, the teacher told her to "stop hollering."

Maybe he didn't know Psalm 47, but Mahalia did. "Shout unto the Lord with the voice of a trumpet." She was going to keep "hollering" for the Lord.

All kinds of people started noticing Mahalia's
singing, like the man from Decca Records.
When she was twenty-five, she made her first
gospel record.

Back home in New Orleans, they heard
her on the jukebox.

In Chicago, she was on the radio.

Mahalia sang for as many people as she could. She knew gospel lifted people up. And when you know something like that, you've got to tell it to the world. So she did.

She was a guest on celebrity TV shows.

When she was thirty-eight, she sang in Carnegie Hall. She couldn't believe it. Such a fancy place. She had goose bumps. When she started singing, the audience got goose bumps, too.

She sang in movies.

She sang for presidents and prime ministers.

But she never did sing in a nightclub.

She performed at the March on Washington,
right before Dr. Martin Luther King Jr. gave his
famous "I Have a Dream" speech.

Mahalia loved those words: I...have...a...dream.

Aunt Bell was right.

Mahalia *was* walking with kings and queens.

After all, she was a queen *herself*...
the Queen of Gospel.

Chronology

1911 Mahalia is born. Her family lives in a shotgun shack so close to the train tracks, the house shakes when trains pass.

1927 Mahalia moves up to Chicago. She's never been there before, and doesn't know what to expect, but she is willing to leave behind everything she knows to take a chance on Chicago. And herself.

1935 Mahalia starts collaborating with Thomas A. Dorsey, the gospel composer.

1937 Mahalia gets her first recording contract, with Decca Records.

1950 Mahalia sings at the world-famous Carnegie Hall as the headlining act at the first Negro Gospel Music Festival.

1954 Mahalia signs with Columbia Records and records *Bless This House*, the first of her thirty albums for the label. Mahalia's Columbia deal includes a national radio show out of Chicago called *The Mahalia Jackson Show*, which is the first all-gospel radio hour.

1956 Mahalia appears on Ed Sullivan's popular television show. Many more people see her sing.

1959 Mahalia has a small acting role in the movie *Imitation of Life*.

1960 Although Mahalia is an international star, her financial success brings racist backlash at home in the Chicago suburbs, where she's purchased a home. She receives violent threats from neighbors who do not want an African American woman living on their street.

1961 Mahalia sings at President John F. Kennedy's inaugural ball.

1963 Mahalia sings at the March on Washington, right before her friend Dr. Martin Luther King Jr. gives his famous "I Have a Dream" speech. Hundreds of thousands of people get to "walk with kings and queens" that day.

1968 Mahalia sings at the funeral of Dr. Martin Luther King Jr. That she is able to sing through that amount of loss is amazing and inspirational.

1972 Mahalia dies, and Dr. Martin Luther King Jr.'s wife, Coretta Scott King, speaks at her funeral. Mahalia also wins the lifetime achievement Grammy Award that year.

1993 The city council of New Orleans votes to honor Mahalia and rename the New Orleans Theater of the Performing Arts. Now it's the Mahalia Jackson Theater for the Performing Arts.

1997 Mahalia is inducted into the Rock and Roll Hall of Fame.

1998 The United States Postal Service issues a commemorative postage stamp to pay respect to Mahalia.

2009 The Mahalia Jackson Theater for the Performing Arts triumphantly reopens its doors after extensive damage from Hurricane Katrina required rebuilding.

More Ways to Learn About Mahalia

Online

In Mahalia's time, they didn't have computers. Now we can go to www.mahaliajackson.us to learn more.

YouTube has video footage of her singing at the March on Washington and at Dr. Martin Luther King Jr.'s funeral.

Library

In addition to CDs of her singing and books about her, the library has a database with a section called "Biography in Context" that has links to magazine articles and other resources. A library card will give you access to this database from any computer.